MW01130506

IN SEARCH OF THE UNEXPLAINED

STONEHENGE

by Jenna Lee Gleisner

Kaleidoscope
Minneapolis, MN

BIGFOOT BOOKS

The Quest for *Discovery* Never Ends

This edition first published in 2022 by Kaleidoscope Publishing, Inc.

For information regarding permission, write to Kaleidoscope Publishing, Inc.
6012 Blue Circle Drive
Minnetonka, MN 55343

Library of Congress Control Number
2021934891

ISBN
978-1-64519-487-3 (library bound)
978-1-64519-525-2 (ebook)

Printed in the United States of America.

FIND ME IF YOU CAN!

Bigfoot lurks within one of the images in this book. It's up to you to find him!

TABLE OF
CONTENTS

STONEHENGE'S SECRETS

As the class nears Salisbury Plain, they can't help but feel excited—and curious. The students have traveled about 90 miles (140 kilometers) from London. They arrive just outside Wiltshire, England. Here on this plain stand the mysterious stones of Stonehenge.

"I heard thousands of dead bodies are buried here!" says one student as they walk up.

"It's just a bunch of stones in a circle. What else could it be?" asks another.

"Aliens built it! They built other henges around here, too. I'm keeping my eyes peeled," says a third. They walk across the green grass. They can't wait to get a better look at the giant stones.

Chapter 1

ANCIENT STONES

Upright and arranged in a circle, roughly 100 **ancient** stones stand in an open field. This circle of stones has left **archaeologists** puzzled for centuries. Who built Stonehenge? How did they move the giant stones? And most importantly, why? Was this a place of worship? Was it a burial site? Maybe it was used as a **solar calendar**. Or maybe it served as a landing site or **portal** for aliens. Could it still today? Decide for yourself as we go in search of the unexplained!

A henge is a circular structure. It is surrounded by a bank or ditch. Standing stones or wooden posts are often part of henges.

Many believe
Stonehenge was built by
humans. They also believe
it was built in stages.
Neolithic Britons are
thought to have started
it more than 5,000 years
ago! Building continued
in stages for about 1,500
years. That's a long time!
But without machines or
any help, this would have
been no easy task. The
wheel wasn't even invented
when builders decided to
move these giant boulders.

FUN FACT
It is estimated that it took more than twenty million hours to build Stonehenge.

WIZARDS AND GIANTS

According to folklore, Merlin the wizard moved the rocks. Legend says giants put them together in Ireland. Then Merlin used his powers to move them to England.

Possible land route
Possible sea route

UNITED
KINGDOM

ENGLAND

WALES

Preseli Hills

Marlborough
Downs

Bristol Channel

STONEHENGE

If human hands really did build it, how did they do it? The largest stones are sarsens. They are about 23 feet (7.0 meters) tall. They weigh up to 30 tons (27,000 kilograms) each! These came from Marlborough Downs, about 20 miles (32 km) away.

The smaller stones are bluestones. They weigh up to five tons (4,500 kg). These have been traced all the way to Preseli Hills. What's odd about this? That's almost 200 miles (320 km) away. How would people have moved these without machines? One **theory** is that they rolled them over tree trunks. Humans would have rolled them the entire distance. But tree trunks would have worn down under all of that weight.

Chapter 2

TRACKING THE SUN

Even more puzzling than how it was built is why. What do the stones mean? They had to be important if so much effort went into moving them. And what about the way they're arranged? Studying how they're placed with an eye to the sky gives us one possible answer.

The upright stones line up with the sun. The entrance points to the rising sun on the summer **solstice**. It points to the sunset on the winter solstice. Were people using the stones as a calendar? Tracking the sun would have helped with farming. It would've let them know what time of year to plant crops and when to harvest them.

STONEHENGE AS A SOLAR CALENDAR

Summer solstice sunset

Summer solstice sunrise

80°

Winter solstice sunset

Winter solstice sunrise

The stones are arranged in a circle. They are evenly spaced as well. This would have required advanced math. What else? Knowledge of the stars and their placement.

Telescopes didn't exist. So how did people line up the stones with the stars so accurately? Some think they followed the sun and stars with the naked eye. Then they modeled the stones after them. But even if it was used as a calendar, why build one so big?

OTHER HENGES

What we see now at Stonehenge is just part of the original structure. Around 20 other henges have been found in the area. Around 70 similar structures stand throughout Britain. Was Stonehenge the center of all of them? Maybe we have yet to figure out the larger picture.

Chapter 3

HONORING THE DEAD

Studying human remains buried here could tell us why this **monument** was so big and important. The items buried with them could also be clues. Stonehenge is thought to be a mass gravesite or burial ground. And it wasn't just any old cemetery.

Gold from other parts of the continent has been found buried with remains. What does this tell us? People traveled thousands of miles to be buried or bury their dead here. And they were very wealthy.

17

A closer look at the
stones may also tell
us this was a place to
honor the dead. Small
axe marks have been
found on stones here.
This marking was used to
mark graves. Also, all of the
stones here had to be shaped.
Those the sunset shines on are more
carefully shaped. This tells us they were probably
meant to mark the winter solstice more than the
summer solstice. The winter solstice marked a time
of death.

SHAPING STONES

Workers had to shape the stones. How did they do this? They used bones, antlers, and other rocks. These tools have been found at the site. They would've been used to chip away, shape, and then smooth the rocks. This would have taken 10 men over 10 years to do.

Chapter 4

ALIEN PORTALS

Some argue that building Stonehenge by hand would have been impossible. But there really isn't any other possible explanation. Or is there? Some believe signs point to **extraterrestrials**. Did aliens build Stonehenge and the other henges?

Who knows the solar system and placement of the stars better than aliens? And who or what would have had the power and advanced **technology** to move giant stones to line up with them?

Even more convincing is the extraterrestrial **phenomena** that take place around Stonehenge. Many people have claimed to see **UFOs** zipping through the sky above Stonehenge and the surrounding area.

FUN FACT

Several thousand UFO sightings have been reported in this area.

Crop circles are also reported here. And not just any crop circles. In 1996 in Wiltshire, a complex mathematical shape was found in a field. This marked one of the most complicated crop circles ever. Were aliens trying to say something? Were they sending information? Some believe the crop circle was more than a message. It could be the answer to opening a portal.

The 1996 Wiltshire crop circle design

LANDING SITE

Stonehenge is in a large, open field. It is big enough to view from space. Clearly visible and with plenty of open space, this could be an ideal place for spacecraft to land.

BLUESTONES

The bluestones here are made of quartz. Quartz has magnetic qualities. It can also change natural electrical movements into energy. This energy increases under weight. The big bluestones would provide plenty of that. Were aliens able to use these energies to create a portal? And are they still using it today?

A bluestone

PLACE OF HEALING

Bluestones are thought to have healing powers. Was Stonehenge a place of healing? Perhaps people came here hoping to heal. Signs of illness and injury have been found in remains buried here.

Stonehenge is arguably Earth's most mysterious ancient monument. It is also one of the most studied and yet we don't have an answer. We know the stones were shaped. We know they were placed thousands of years ago. But no written records of its creation exist. And the builders left few clues behind.

Did aliens create Stonehenge? Was or is it a landing site or portal? Did human hands build it as a place of **ritual**? Was it a burial ground or place to honor the dead? What purpose do you think these stones served?

BEYOND THE BOOK

After reading the book, it's time to think about what you learned. Try the following exercises to jump-start your ideas.

THINK

FIND OUT MORE. There is so much more to dig up about Stonehenge. What do you want to learn? Look up sightings at Stonehenge on the web, or check out a book from the library. What explanations can you find?

CREATE

ART TIME. Can you draw Stonehenge? Look up a picture and grab some markers and paper. Will a person see something there? Will there be any clues? The sky is the limit!

SHARE

THE MORE WHO KNOW. Share what you learned about Stonehenge. Use your own words to write a paragraph. What are the main ideas of this book? What facts from the book can you use to support those ideas? Share your paragraph with a classmate. Do they have any comments or questions?

GROW

DISCOVER! The universe is so large. There could be anything out there. Find a group or watch the stars with your family. If you can, bring a telescope and a star map. Space holds so much to discover!

RESEARCH NINJA

Visit *www.ninjaresearcher.com/4873* to learn how to take your research skills and book report writing to the next level!

Research

DIGITAL LITERACY TOOLS

SEARCH LIKE A PRO
Learn how to use search engines to find useful websites.

FACT OR FAKE
Discover how you can tell a trusted website from an untrustworthy resource.

TEXT DETECTIVE
Explore how to zero in on the information you need most.

SHOW YOUR WORK
Research responsibly—learn how to cite sources.

Write

DOWNLOADABLE BOOK REPORT FORMS

GET TO THE POINT
Learn how to express your main ideas.

PLAN OF ATTACK
Learn prewriting exercises and create an outline.

FURTHER RESOURCES

BOOKS

Coddington, Andrew. *The Bermuda Triangle, Stonehenge, and Unexplained Places*. New York: Cavendish Square Publishing, 2018.

Peterson, Megan Cooley. *Stonehenge: Who Built this Stone Formation?* Mankato, Minn.: Black Rabbit Books, 2019.

York, M.J. *12 Ancient Mysteries*. North Mankato, Minn.: 12-Story Library, 2017.

WEBSITES

FACTSURFER

Factsurfer.com gives you a safe, fun way to find more information.

1. Go to www.factsurfer.com.

2. Enter "Stonehenge" into the search box and click 🔍

3. Select your book cover to see a list of related websites.

GLOSSARY

ancient: belonging to a period long ago.

archaeologists: people who study the distant past. Archaeologists often dig up old items and examine them carefully.

extraterrestrials: beings from outer space or another world.

folklore: the stories, customs, and beliefs of common people that are handed down from one generation to the next.

legend: a story handed down from earlier times. Legends are often based on fact, but they are not entirely true.

monument: a statue, building, or structure that reminds people of an event or person.

Neolithic: of or relating to the latest period of the Stone Age.

phenomena: rare, remarkable, and significant events.

portal: an entrance, especially a large or important one.

prehistoric: belonging to a time before history was recorded in written form.

ritual: an act or series of acts that are performed in the same way, usually as part of a religious or social ceremony.

solar calendar: a calendar whose dates point to seasons and the position of the sun.

solstices: the longest and shortest days of the year.

technology: the use of science and engineering to do or build something.

telescopes: instruments that make distant objects look larger and closer. Telescopes are used especially for studying the stars and other heavenly bodies.

theory: an idea or statement that explains how or why something happens.

UFO: an object that is seen flying in the sky and that some people believe is a spacecraft from another planet. UFO is short for unidentified flying object.

PHOTO CREDITS

The images in this book are reproduced through the courtesy of: Pecold/Shutterstock Images, p. cover; Andrew Roland/Shutterstock Images, p. 3; Grumpy and Curious/Shutterstock Images, p. 4; Ruediger Nold/Shutterstock Images, p. 5; Patrick Foto/Shutterstock Images, p. 6 (kid); Orion Media Group/Shutterstock Images, p. 6 (stones), 30; Nicholas Grey/Shutterstock Images, p. 7; Roni Setiawan/Shutterstock Images, p. 8 (top); Lightspring/Shutterstock Images, p. 8 (bottom); Digital Storm/Shutterstock Images, p. 9; SherSS/Shutterstock Images, p. 11; Chuta Kooanantkul/ Shutterstock Images, p. 12; Nerthuz/Shutterstock Images, p. 13 (sun); PTZ Pictures/Shutterstock Images, p. 14 (top); Zieusin/Shutterstock Images, p. 14 (bottom); Triff/Shutterstock Images, p. 15 (top); Richard Hayman/Shutterstock Images, p. 15 (bottom); Eoghan McNally/Shutterstock Images, p. 16 (top); DeStefano/Shutterstock Images, p. 16 (bottom); Microgen/Shutterstock Images, p. 17 (top); Maria Kovalets/Shutterstock Images, p. 17 (bottom); MaP9999/Shutterstock Images, p. 18 (circle); Andrew Roland/Shutterstock Images, p. 18 (bottom); Juan Aunion/Shutterstock Images, p. 19 (top); Wlad74/Shutterstock Images, p. 19 (bottom left); Prapann/Shutterstock Images, p. 19 (right); Adike/ Shutterstock Images, p. 20; DanieleGay/Shutterstock Images, p. 21; Helen Hotson/Shutterstock Images, p. 22 (circle); FFMR/Shutterstock Images, p. 22 (bottom); PTZ Pictures/Shutterstock Images, p. 23 (top); WesAbrams/iStockphoto, p. 23 (bottom); Drone Explorer/Shutterstock Images, p. 24 (top); Capitolio Arts/Shutterstock Images, p. 24 (bottom); Nikki Zalewski/Shutterstock Images, p. 25; Valentyna Chukhlyebova/Shutterstock Images, p. 26 (alien); Roberto La Rosa/Shutterstock Images, p. 26-27; DeStefano/Shutterstock Images, p. 27 (circle).

ABOUT THE AUTHOR

Jenna Lee Gleisner is a children's book author and editor who lives in Minnesota. In her spare time, she likes to hike, read, research fun topics like Bigfoot, and spend time with her dog, Norrie.